The Healing Process

CASSANDRA WADE

WESTBOW®
PRESS
A DIVISION OF THOMAS NELSON
& ZONDERVAN

WestBow Press books may be ordered through
booksellers or by contacting:

WestBow Press
A Division of Thomas Nelson & Zondervan
1663 Liberty Drive
Bloomington, IN 47403
www.westbowpress.com
1 (866) 928-1240

Because of the dynamic nature of the Internet, any web
addresses or links contained in this book may have changed
since publication and may no longer be valid. The views
expressed in this work are solely those of the author and do
not necessarily reflect the views of the publisher, and the
publisher hereby disclaims any responsibility for them.

Any people depicted in stock imagery provided
by Thinkstock are models, and such images are
being used for illustrative purposes only.
Certain stock imagery © Thinkstock.

ISBN: 978-1-4908-4209-7 (sc)
ISBN: 978-1-4908-4211-0 (hc)
ISBN: 978-1-4908-4210-3 (e)

Library of Congress Control Number: 2014911310

Printed in the United States of America.

WestBow Press rev. date: 06/19/2014

This book is dedicated to those who have lost loved ones due to cancer. I pray that one day there will be a cure. I feel your pain, and I know what you are going through. I pray that this book will help you find peace and comfort and know that God is still doing miracles.

Contents

Introduction

We all have dreams. I'm not talking about dreams at night when we fall asleep. I'm referring to the dream of success or achievement. God has given us something to do on this earth. We all have to meet those expectations, and God will make sure this will happen. My dream was to raise my son, get a decent job, and take care of my mother, such as paying bills and just helping her out. Little did I know that things would not be the same after 2005. What a wake-up call I had. God had a plan for me that was bigger than I could ever imagine.

My mother passed in 2005, which left me depressed and saw me turn my back on God. My mom always told me that God would not put more on me than I could bear, but I felt that life had cheated me of my mother. I was twenty-seven at the time. I had my whole life ahead of me but didn't know or care what happen to anyone. I prayed and prayed to God for my mother's healing but instead, she passed. What a devastating blow.

God will put us in situations just to test us. I think this was my biggest test of all, because I had stopped praying. There were times when I couldn't even talk to God, and there were times when I couldn't face life. I felt I couldn't go on. Friends talked to me and checked on me, but they couldn't imagine how I was feeling because they still had their mothers with them. I figured that no one—not even

God—could help me, because I'd made up my mind to do it my way. I didn't realize that God was still right there with me.

In this book, I will go into detail on certain events in my life and how I began to pray again and believe there was a God who still loved me and cared for me, regardless of my flaws. While I was trying to figure out how I was going to make it, God was waiting on me to make that move. In reality, my dreams and desires that I once had would soon come to pass.

Every time I'm faced with a challenge that I can't handle by myself, I leave it to God. What a mighty God I serve.

1

Colon Cancer Life and Death Issues

Colon cancer, also called colorectal cancer, is one the most common cancers in women and men. My mother died from colorectal cancer.

Until my mom was diagnosed, I had not heard of colorectal cancer. There was no prior family history of colorectal cancer, but my mom's diagnosis made me aware of how important it is to know about this disease.

I had my first colonoscopy in 2008. It went well, though I was a little sore and had some stomach pain after the procedure. But the doctor said my colon looked good.

My second colonoscopy was in 2013. I will get one every five years. I'm not looking for a problem with my health; I'm being more aware of my health. I have a family history of high blood pressure, diabetes, heart disease, and high cholesterol, as well as colorectal cancer.

With all of this in my family history, I get a checkup every year that includes a breast exam. All of my exams have come back with good results. I suggest that everyone learn what's in his or her family history. Having this information, can put you one step ahead of the process. Knowing your family history or even making a family tree will provide you with details on the health of each generation.

If colorectal cancer is caught in time, it can be treated. The best way to catch the disease is with regular checkups. Don't wait until any symptoms get out of control and the disease has spread.

A colonoscopy is a simple procedure, but the preparation for it starts at home. The day before my procedure, I couldn't eat anything after noon, and I had to drink a laxative solution—it's flavored, but it still tasted unpleasant. This solution helped to empty my bowels so my doctor could view my colon.

The next step was the procedure itself. During a colonoscopy, my doctor used a narrow tube with a light and camera on one end, called a scope, to look inside the rectum and the entire colon. He looked for polyps or growths in the rectum or colon.

A colonoscopy is an outpatient procedure, so I returned home after it was over. The doctor gave my report to the person who brought me to the office that day because I was still under sedation.

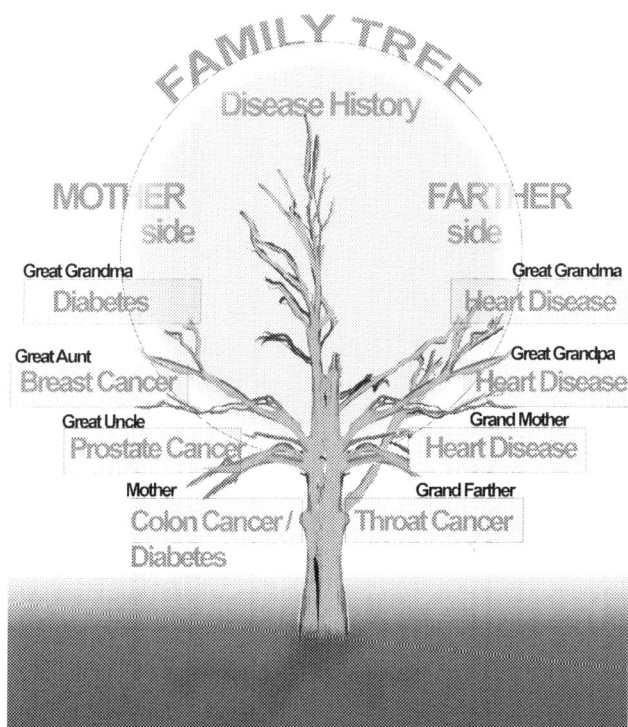

FAMILY TREE

Disease History

MOTHER side

FARTHER side

Great Grandma
Diabetes

Great Grandma
Heart Disease

Great Aunt
Breast Cancer

Great Grandpa
Heart Disease

Great Uncle
Prostate Cancer

Grand Mother
Heart Disease

Mother
Colon Cancer / Throat Cancer
Diabetes

Grand Farther

2

Memories for a Lifetime

My mother worked hard to provide a happy life for her eight children. She was there to help and give advice, and she did it all without any strife.

The memories of my mother, Cassandra Williams, will never be forgotten, and no one can replace them. I have special memories of my mother from when I was a kid. She was a single parent of four girls and four boys, and never once did she complain about what we didn't have or how hard it was to be a single mother. She did what it took to make sure all eight of her children were well taken care of.

My mother was a certified nursing assistant who worked from 3:00 to 11:00 p.m. Sometimes she worked two shifts, just to make ends meet and make sure we had clothes, food, and shelter. Working two shifts wasn't easy. I remember her coming home, her feet sore from standing or walking nonstop, and her back in so much pain from lifting her patients. At one point, she hurt her back on the job and needed back surgery. But even back surgery didn't stop her.

When I was in middle and high school, Mom made sure dinner was cooked before she went to work, and she would call often while she was at work to make sure we did our chores and homework and had our clothes ironed for the next day. Bedtime was at 8:00 p.m. for the younger kids and 9:30 p.m. for the oldest. Everything had to be done by the time she got off work, or she would wake us up when she got home—and that was something we didn't want, because she would wake us up with the belt. So we did everything.

On Sundays, all eight of us kids were in church. We didn't miss a Sunday or Bible study on Wednesday nights. Even though we would attend church on Sundays and Wednesdays, we still had a Bible lesson at home. We were expected to choose a Bible verse and explain what it meant to us. If we couldn't explain, we had to teach a Bible lesson or read a whole chapter in the Bible and then write one page about what we read.

My siblings and I would make fun of whoever had to write or teach a lesson, but my mom made the one who laughed at that person teach a lesson for two weeks and write on what we talked about, to see whether it matched up with what we said in the lesson. We might stray from our faith, but her teaching will forever be with us.

Even when she worked two shifts, my mother always made time for us, especially when we had something going on at school. Sore feet, hurting back, and all, she was there, cheering us on.

As we became adults and started having kids of our own, she was there at the hospital, before and after the births. And with her grandchildren, for any special events at their schools, she was there, cheering them on.

My son was the first grandchild, and she would volunteer at his school or stand in for me when I had to work. Even after she became ill, my mother attended different activities at the grandkids' schools and was involved in their lives. During the times when she was in the hospital for weeks, she wanted me to tell her how everyone was doing, from the oldest to the youngest. She had a special bond with each of us.

Even when my mother was going through chemotherapy, she always had a smile on her face and never once complained about anything. She thanked God at all times. My mother stood in faith through sickness, pain, and going back and forth to the hospital. She encouraged others with whom she came in contact who were facing difficult situations. She praised her God and visited other churches. She put on musicals, took care of her family, and participated in educational organizations, her children's school activities, and church activities.

My mother had a generous spirit that was sensitive to God. Her sister Susan also had strong faith in God. Susan agreed with my mother about many different problems and circumstances that the devil brought her way.

In 1988, when I was ten years old, my mother was excited about her pregnancy exam, which revealed she was carrying twins. She called to tell my aunt Susan about it, and Susan shouted with joy. Immediately, the Holy Spirit spoke to my aunt Susan that my mother was having twin girls. My mother hoped this was so because the doctor had told my mother that she was going to have twin boys. As it turned out, she had twin girls.

During her seventh month of pregnancy, my mother went into labor. One girl weighed 1 pound 13 ounces, and the other girl weighed 1 pound 12 ounces. They were about the size of a man's hand. They were placed in incubators, and the light from the lamps caused their skin to peel. The doctor told my mother that my sisters weren't going to make it.

My church family and my aunt Susan, through their prayers, declared life and divine health over my twin sisters every day. They agreed with my mother that God moved on their behalf to give them a miracle. The doctor was convinced that my sisters wouldn't make it through the night or through the week, but they said if the twins did survive, they wouldn't be able to walk, talk, see, or have children, and they would be mentally retarded.

God pulled down all those lies from the Devil. My mother stood in faith, believing and trusting in God, like always.

The social workers, with the doctor's approval, wanted to send the babies to New Orleans to be in therapy there indefinitely. Again, prayers went up because no matter how often my mother asked them to keep her babies with her in Shreveport, the doctor refused and told her the helicopters were going to pick up the girls on a certain day, and that was the end of it. When that day arrived, my mother left the hospital so she wouldn't have to see her babies leave and go on a journey away from home. Even though my mother went home, she still believed in God.

When the helicopter arrived at the hospital, however, the staff took two other babies to New Orleans instead of my mother's babies.

My mother was excited and overjoyed. She had stood on the Word of God and believed in a miracle. Her faith didn't waiver during those months as the twins developed in mind, body, and soul. God showed up and showed out on her behalf many times.

Is there anything too hard for God? God was real to my mother. She trusted God to take care of her family. She went through school by faith and cared for her children, house, and church. She was truly a woman who believed in the power of God and stood on the Word until it manifested. My mother was definitely a woman of faith.

In 2003, I was five months pregnant but had a miscarriage. I needed a dilation and curettage (D&C) to remove tissue in the uterus. After this procedure, I got sick. I could hardly walk, eat, or breathe and was in a lot of pain.

When the doctor examined me, he found out that during the D&C, some of the afterbirth was left in me. I returned to the hospital for a second D&C, and this time I ended up getting pneumonia and had to be placed in the intensive care unit for a week. While I was in the hospital, my mom took the responsibility of taking care of my son, and she would be at the hospital with me all the time as well. I couldn't get up and bathe, so she took on that responsibility and bathed me. She acted like my nurse. She was constantly praying over me. I remember the doctor told my mom that I had become so ill that I might not live. My mom told the doctor that God had the last say on that. "My daughter is going to get well," she told them.

As a child and an adult, I don't ever think my mother's faith ever waivered, even through her sickness. My mother went through many ups and downs in her life, but God was with her, every step of the way.

My mother taught me that no matter how hard it gets, I can manage. I find myself doing exactly the same thing with my son. When I get off work, I cook, check homework, iron clothes for school, and get chores done. Bedtime is at 9:30, and church is every Sunday and sometimes on Wednesday night for Bible study.

Thanks, Mom, for teaching me and helping me understand that there's nobody stronger than a single parent. Just like my mom, I do what I do to make sure my son has what he needs and that he's loved, protected, and cared for. The memories of my mom and the love she gave will never be forgotten.

3

Where It All Began

It began like a regular Sunday. We went to church, came home, and Mom cooked dinner. After that, we sat around laughing and talking, just having a good time, as we always did. Later on that day, Mom kept complaining of stomach pains. We didn't think too much of it, because we assumed it had to do with something she had eaten. Little did we know that it really was something serious.

I will never forget the moment that evening when my mom came out the restroom and said, "I have blood in my stool."

I told her, "Come Monday, we need to go get this checked out."

My mother agreed but then said, "Right now, let's pray and turn this around, and give it to God."

So we prayed and praised God. It's good to pray and believe and have that personal relationship with God. God also gave us a physician for Mom to see. Matthew 9:12 says, "They that are whole need not a physician, but they that are sick."

And yes, my mother got to the point where she was sick and would not go to the doctor. I begged her, and when she finally went, the doctor couldn't find the cause for this problem. She kept receiving pints of blood, but somehow, the next week or so she needed more blood. Finally, the doctor found that she had colon cancer.

My mom had all the symptoms related to colon cancer. Mayo Clinic lists the symptoms of colon cancer on its website (mayoclinic. com/health/colon-cancer):

- A change in your bowel habits, including diarrhea or constipation or a change in the consistency of your stool
- Rectal bleeding or blood in your stool
- Persistent abdominal discomfort, such as cramps, gas, or pain
- A feeling that your bowel doesn't empty completely
- Weakness or fatigue
- Unexplained weight loss

According to the Mayo Clinic, "Many people with colon cancer experience no symptoms in the early stages of the disease. When symptoms appear, they'll likely vary, depending on the cancer's size and location in your large intestine."

My mother had all these symptoms. Sometimes when my mother had a bowel movement, it would come out as little round balls. This was not normal at all.

When the doctor told my mother that she had colon cancer, he told her it was best if she had the surgery, but she could do what she wanted to do. My mom told me what the doctor had said but then said she had decided to pray about it and give it to God because she really didn't want the doctor cutting her. As the days went by and she continued praying, something burst on the inside of her, and she expelled it like running water. The smell of it was awful. She got a big white towel to stop the flow, and we rushed her to the hospital.

Before going into surgery, we prayed that God would be with her and that the surgery would go well. Surgery lasted about five hours. When the doctor spoke to me after the surgery, he said he'd removed the majority of the cancer but could not get it all. "She's lucky to be alive," he said. "You can see her after the nurse puts her in recovery."

All I could say was, "Thank you, God. My mother will make it through this." I stayed at the hospital until she was put into a room, and then I went home and got ready for work.

The next day, Mom called me to ask what the doctor had said. I really did not want to tell her, but she said, "Tell me. I can handle it." After I repeated the doctor's words, my mother said, "I trust God. My life is in God's hands."

My mom never stopped believing and trusting in God. Her favorite saying was, "I believe in God." My mom stayed in the hospital for four days. She came home the day before Thanksgiving and was determined to cook—and she did, with my sister's and my help. We had a great Thanksgiving, not knowing that 2004 would be the last.

After my mom got well, she started to move around again and was back to her old self. My mom was always on the go. She was always doing something, and she didn't let this cancer or chemotherapy stop her. If I was not at work, we were together; she was my best friend. Life isn't the same without her, but I thank God for giving me a caring, loving mother. No matter what happened, she would always have the right words to say.

Three weeks after the surgery, Mom began her chemotherapy treatments. I was there every time she took her treatments. She would go on Friday, between noon and two thirty. After that, she would be sick for the next three days, then feel better, but then go back again on the following Friday to start over again. Mom would be so sick from taking the treatments that she would constantly throw up. She couldn't keep any food down at all. I always thought the chemo treatments did not help her, because Mom was always sick after taking them.

After a year or so, she would get a shot instead of the treatments. This would take place on Sunday before going to church. She would go in to the doctor's office, and it would take at least ten minutes to get the shot. Then off to church we would go. I thought many times that the chemo would shrink or do away with the cancer, but it wasn't doing anything but making her sick; this would happen every single time.

I might be wrong, but chemo is a killer not for the cancer but for that person who receives it. I heard a doctor say at one time that chemo is the only cancer treatment needed. It is part of the treatment plan that can include surgery, so it can shrink cancer or be used with other treatments if the cancer comes back. With my mom, we thought it was working because one minute she was sick and the next, she was doing good.

I thought chemo would cure her cancer, but I never thought that the goal was to slow the growth of cancer or reduce symptoms. It just seemed like it wasn't doing its job, which was the hardest part for my mother and me.

I thanked God for the uncommon favor he showed me throughout this process of my life. There were many times when Mom felt like giving up, but she was willing to fight to the end. She never stopped believing in God for her healing. When my mother was going through this ordeal, her favorite saying was, "Don't give up on me. I believe in God for my healing."

God did heal her—not in the way I wanted him to do, but he did heal her. I would always go in my room alone and pray, asking God to take the pain away from my mom and please heal her. I would repeat this prayer over and over, every day. I had to learn to stop telling God what I wanted and start accepting his will for our lives. I wanted my mom here with me, but at the same time, she was suffering, and that was something I did not like to see. I guess my prayer should have been, "God, let your will be done."

Bowed-Down Head

With my head down, tears in my eyes, the pain won't go away.

With my head, down tears in my eyes, while hope faded away.

With my head, down tears in my eyes, I lost all faith.

With my head down, tears in my eyes, waiting for a better day.

With my head down, tears in my eyes, I'm drowning in sorrow.

With my head down, tears in my eyes, my heart is broken.

With my head down, tears in my eyes, my heart is too heavy to bear the loss.

With my head down, tears in my eyes, can I ever look up again?

With my head down, tears in my eyes, the more I prayed the worst I got.

With my head down, tears in my eyes, the more I wish I forgot.

With my head down, tears in my eyes, as I get ready to close the door, I learned to lean on Revelation 21:4.

"He will wipe every tear from their eyes, and death shall be no more, neither shall there be mourning, nor crying, nor pain anymore, for the former things have passed away."

4

Mother's Death and Family

Mom, your love will continue to live forever in our hearts.

My mother's last days were spent sleeping all the time due to the medication her doctor had prescribed. I was living with her, and there were times when I didn't get any sleep because she would wake up screaming in pain, or I'd have to change her colostomy bag. The smell was horrible, but I was willing to do anything for my mom. (The colostomy bag was necessary after Mom's surgery. It attached to an opening on her stomach to collect waste on the outside of her body.) I would empty the colostomy bag every thirty minutes to an hour because it would get so full. I felt like I was her nurse because I made sure she was well taken care of, along with the other nurses.

My aunt Susan also helped. She would take my mother to her doctor's appointment and make sure that she was looked after. My mom best friend, Debra, prayed for her and also took her to her doctor's appointment and to chemo. She did whatever she could and made sure that Mom was looked after—this also included the rest of my family. Sylvia Larkin's family was there as well and were a big help to my mother. I am grateful to everyone who played a major role with my mother while she was going through her sickness.

In October 2005, my mom went to the hospital, but they sent her home, because there was nothing else that they could do for her. Hospice got involved, and a young man named J. came by the house and prayed with her and made sure she was okay. My mom was on a lot of medication: Cipro, Actigall, OxyContin, Phenergan, Megace, Senokot, Metformin, and Bactrim. Some of the medicine was for Mom's diabetes and gallstones, but she was taking five or six different medications a day to ease her pain. She developed jaundice in both of her eyes due to a problem with her liver. Through all her pain and illness, she still believed in God for her healing.

It seemed like the medicine had stopped working and her condition worsened. There was nothing else for the doctor to do. My mom's last hospital stay had been on September 30, 2005. The doctor wanted to keep her longer, but she wanted to come home and be around her kids. We didn't know that eight days later, she would be gone.

After she came home from the hospital, she slept most of the time, but on October 5, 2005, she kept repeating these words: "God forgive me. God forgive me. Thank you, God, for all things you have done for me." She began to sing "Have Your Way" by Joe Pace, which includes the repetition of the line "Have your way, have your way, have your way," and ends with the words, "To your will, to your way, I will go, yes I'll obey."

After singing this song, she began to cry and said, "Thank you, God," which she kept repeating until she went back to sleep. I didn't know this at first, but she was getting herself right with God, something we all must do before we meet our heavenly Father. I really didn't catch on to why she was saying that, because I believed in God for her healing, and I just knew God was going to heal my mother. The thought never came across my mind that she was getting herself right with God, and she was giving up.

The rest of the day, she slept until it was time to take her medicine. She had stopped eating by this time. The only thing she would take by mouth was ice; it was the only thing her stomach could tolerate. I would try to make her eat, and sometimes she would and sometimes she would not. Most of the time, she threw up greenish liquid.

On October 7, 2005, a Friday night, I slept on the couch, but I really didn't get any sleep. I was up with my mom because she was screaming in pain. I was so upset because I couldn't do anything at all but hold her hand and pray to God that the pain would go away. The medicine had stopped working; nothing was working. I knew Mom was hurting because when she held my hand, she had a tight grip on it,

At one point that night, my mom woke up and said, "I see my new home." I didn't understand what she was talking about until she passed. Whatever she was seeing, it was beautiful because she was smiling as she went back to sleep. This would happen again throughout the night.

I finally went to sleep around two thirty the morning of October 8, 2005, but I couldn't really sleep. I would wake up repeatedly to make sure my mom was okay. I finally woke up around 5:00 a.m. to get ready for work; I had to be there at six. As I was getting ready for work, my mom woke up, and we began to talk. She let me know that if she had to go back to the hospital, she wanted me to come. I told her I would be there, even if I had to leave work early.

When I was going out the door that morning, Mom called my name and said, "Don't forget—if I have to go back to the hospital, I need you there, because you are on top of things."

Again, I said I would be there. And she thanked me for being there for her, for holding her hand, and for praying for her. Then she said, "Thank you for staying up with me. I know you didn't get any sleep before work."

I responded, "You are my mother. I would not have it any other way. I will be calling to check on you, and I will get off work early. I love you." I did not know that this was the last time I would talk with her.

I went to work. During that time I was working as a waitress and had to open up and get things ready for the customers for seven thirty breakfast. I really couldn't work, because my mind was on my mother, but I tried to get my mind off the situation by throwing myself into work. Still, every thirty minutes I called home to check on my mother, just as I had promised.

My brother answered the phone when I called. He said Mom was sleeping, and he gave the same report every thirty minutes until around 11:30 a.m. When I called that time, I heard a lot of noise, and I asked what was going on. That's when my brother told me that Mom was unconscious, and they were trying to wake her up. It still didn't click in my head until I called back again, and this time, he said, "She's not breathing. She's not responding. Aunt Susan is doing CPR on her."

I screamed through the phone at my brother to call 911. And then I told him I would call back in another thirty minutes—it still hadn't clicked that he was trying to tell me that my mother was gone.

I'd been making the phone calls that morning from the restroom, and as I came out of the restroom this time, planning on telling the manager that I had to go home, I looked up and saw Sylvia Larkin. She took me by the hand, and all she said was, "Come on. We have to go."

And I knew then that my mom was gone. I started to scream, and everyone, from my coworkers to my manager, ran up to me to find out what was going on. I remember that Sylvia told my manager that my mom was dead. Sylvia physically had to put me in the car. I couldn't stop screaming as she put my seat belt on me, and we headed to my house. I remember Sylvia's telling me, "Calm down. We're almost there."

When we arrived, I got out the car and ran into the house. Mom was lying on the floor, looking like she was just sleeping. My aunt Susan was crying, and she said she had tried to bring Mom back, but she was already gone. We waited for my other siblings to arrive before the coroner took my mother's body. I wanted to make sure all her kids were there.

After the coroner took my mom's body, a lot of people came over to see how we were doing and to see if we needed anything. After everyone left, I keep questioning my brother,

"Are you sure you did all you could?" Then I would tell him to repeat the details again. He indulged me and repeated about five times the same thing he'd told me on the phone.

I asked my son, "Did your grandmother wake up and say anything?"

He said, "Yes, she asked for some ice, and I got her some, and she went back to sleep."

I went into my room slammed the door. I was crying and kept saying, "Why didn't someone try harder to save her?" I couldn't believe Mom was gone.

My childhood friend came to sit with me for about three hours. She talked to me, but all I could do was cry. Nothing that anyone would say helped because I remembered telling my mom that I would be there for her, that I would get off work early to be with her. It seemed like I'd let her down, and I didn't even get to say good-bye. This just tore me up inside. It seemed like my life wasn't worth living anymore. All I could remember was the promise I'd given her that morning to be there for her.

I asked myself if was I a good daughter. I should have stayed at home. I blamed myself for a lot of things, mainly not being there and not saying good-bye. Why did this happen to me? I asked God several times, "Why my mother? Why, God, why?" I had prayed for my mother and had quoted the same Scripture over and over again. "But he was wounded for our transgressions, he was bruised for our iniquities: the chastisement of our peace was upon him; and with his stripes we are healed" (Isaiah 53:5 KJV). I quoted this for her to get well but instead, I was overruled, and that was something I could not understand. I was angry to the point of giving up.

I never thought that October 8, 2005, would be the end of Mom's life, but I knew my life had ended also. There were many times after that day that I thought about committing suicide. I got to the point where I was ready to give up just because my mom was no longer here. I had turned my back on God.

Many people later told me that it never should have reached that point, and I would tell those people, "You cannot understand unless you have traveled down that same path."

I hadn't minded taking care of my mother while she was sick. I knew that she had made sure all eight of her children would not go without and the same for her grandchildren. My mother gave us security and love. She played two roles: father and mother. She was our everything, and she always put us first, no matter what. Nobody was more important to her than her children. We never went without, even if she had to borrow she made sure we had what we needed. As children and as adults, we never felt unimportant or unloved.

And when my mother passed, it felt like our number-one fan had died. On October 9, 2005, I went to church, and when I came home, I just knew my mom was there ... but I came home to an empty house that still had her scent. Once again, I broke down and cried. I just couldn't believe she was gone. Later that day, we had a family meeting, getting ready to make funeral arguments. In the midst of everything, it was brought to our attention that everyone knew about Mom's condition except us kids. Everyone else, including other family members, knew that she was dying and that the cancer had spread. I was so hurt to learn this. It seemed like it was a big secret that my mother didn't want us to find out. I wish somebody would have told us sooner, instead of waiting until after she died. As time went on, however, I came to understand why this information was kept from the kids.

On Monday, October 10, 2005, I went back to work. I could not bear to stay at home. I had to get out the house. Even though I went back to work and was smiling on the outside, I was hurting on the inside. I had to put on a fake smile for my customers. I didn't want my customers to know that my mother had passed, because I was tired of hearing "I'm sorry for your loss" or "I know what you are going through." I did not want to hear those words; I just wanted to be left alone to deal with it on my own.

It had gotten to the point where I stopped praying. After work, I'd go home and be angry with everyone, including my siblings. I knew my anger got to the point that no one wanted to be around me, and I understood that because I didn't want to be around myself. I just wanted to end my life. After all I'd prayed for the healing of my mother, and she passed anyway. I was crushed to the point that I felt there was no need to pray. I figured, *Why pray when I get no results?* At the time, I couldn't understand. All I wanted was my mother back to her old self.

I often asked God why he couldn't have taken someone else instead of my mother. My mother was the type of person who would do anything for others and pray for those who were sick or going through difficult times. I really couldn't grasp why she had to die.

The viewing of my mother's body was on October 14, 2005, and the hardest thing I had to do was walk in the room. It felt like she was waiting for me and my siblings to get there. I broke down crying, still thinking, "This is a nightmare. This is not true," but of course it was. I just stared at her, and it was as if she would wake up at anytime. Of course she didn't.

I still didn't believe my mom was gone until October 15, 2005, the day of her funeral. My mom was dressed all in blue. Her casket was lined with white and blue, and on the inside of her casket was a white dove with the written message: "We will meet again."

This was the beginning of truth for me. This was the day for me to face the reality that she was really gone. After everything was said and done, I still couldn't believe it was real. I spent many nights crying myself to sleep, and there were many days when I felt like dying myself. I couldn't accept that from then on, I would wake up without seeing my mother's face. I wouldn't see that smile or listen to her sing or even pray.

The only time I would smile was at work, because I had to do so for my customers. But on the inside, I was hurting, and the pain would not go away. I felt like life had cheated me out of so much. I tried to stay strong for my siblings and my son, but at times, I couldn't.

Time went on, but I was still grieving. Then I met a man at work. He was there for me during this time in my life when I'd stopped praying. I was seeking other ways to find comfort, and as long as he was there,

I was okay. I had someone to talk to, even though I was still trying to cover up the hurt, the crying, and the pain I felt. This man and I went out every night, just having a good time and drinking—which I rarely do, but I did it so I would not have to think about the pain of losing my mother. I was drowning in sorrow, wishing and hoping that it was a dream or that someone was playing a trick on me. It was a reality, but as long I didn't have to face the pain, I didn't care. I put this man before God, because I felt that God had overlooked me by not answering my prayers.

It seemed like the more I prayed, the worse I felt. This man, however, was there to listen and to comfort me. In truth, he was there to see what he could get or how he could play with my emotions, but I didn't see that at the time. Everything in that relationship was going well, and I felt that he could relate to me, as his dad also had colon cancer. I buried myself in work and our relationship, which I thought at the time was good. This relationship lasted five years, until I called it off.

I learned a lot from that relationship, such as don't date while grieving, because that person may use that situation against you just to play with your emotions and feelings. It was easy for him to do this because I was at a bad time in my life and couldn't tell up from down. I was trying to cover the pain, knowing that after this relationship ended, I would be back at square one, which was the pain of losing someone who meant the world to me.

The harder I prayed, the worse it got. It seemed like I couldn't see my way. I had to raise my twin sisters and my son. I just couldn't believe all of this was left on me—at the time,

I was only twenty-seven, and it felt like a lot of responsibility. Other family members didn't help, once they realized there wasn't any money to give away—I guess that when the separation began. Through it all, however, my siblings and I learned to stand on our own, regardless of who was against us or whatever situation we had to face.

My siblings and I stayed together a little while after the death of our mother—at least we tried. We eventually had to separate, but we always made sure we called each other, just to say hello or I love you. The most hurtful thing for my siblings and me was coping with holidays and birthdays and family traditions— Thanksgiving was six weeks after my mom passed, and the void once again appeared, but this time, it was more intense than ever, due to the fact we felt anger, depression, guilt, and most of all, loneliness.

My siblings and I missed the holiday cooking that normally would have taken place that day, as well as sitting around laughing and talking. Christmas came around, and it too was worse because my mom would have had the tree up, gifts under the tree, and the Christmas lights up. The majority of the gifts would have been for her grandchildren—she made sure of that. Yes, she spoiled them all.

My siblings and I still struggle to get through the holidays every year. We hate to be reminded of the celebrations we once shared—that is the hardest part. Mother's Day is particularly painful. I remember the last Mother's Day with my mother in 2005. She got up early that morning to make breakfast for my sister and me before I went to work.

She made sure we had the best Mother's Day. Of course, her children treated her like the queen she was. Mother's Day has not been the same since her passing. To me, it's just another day to be reminded of what we once shared and another day without my mom.

The pain of losing her has not eased. I miss the wonderful relationship I once had with her. I miss our talks and her advice. She was my biggest supporter. Her death brought an overwhelming amount of grief. No holidays, birthdays, or family traditions will ever be the same. I'd give all that I own to have her back with me. The pain never fades. I'm still missing my mother.

5

Life after Death

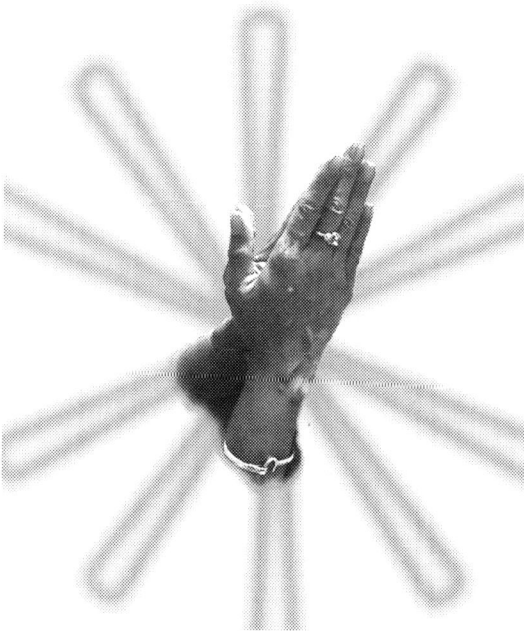

On the day that my mother died, I wished that the earth would open up and swallow me. I was broken and felt so empty on the inside. With all the hurt, pain, and guilt, I still had to get back to my life. Getting back to the routine of work after my mother's passing was very hard, but it was even harder to go home after work when she wasn't there. I would pick up extra shifts at work so I didn't have to face the fact that my mother was no longer living. Of course, I didn't have a choice. I still had responsibilities at home, such as taking care of my son and teenage sisters. My sisters had three more years in high school, and I felt it was my responsibility to make sure they did it since they now were in my care.

Raising teenagers was hard, and I didn't know if I could do it, but somebody had to, and it was me. I know they felt that I was strict and that they barely could do anything. I know at times they felt like they couldn't go on, and I had to play the role of mother to them. That was hard for me because I had to be strict with them and deal with their behaviors. They were just being young ladies, growing up without their mother, and they had to listen to me, their sister. I know they got tired of my fussing and telling them what to do and what not to do, we got through it. If I had to do it over again, I would.

We all went through major changes, especially my sisters. I know they didn't expect it—neither did I—but they finished high school in 2008, They went on to have children and get married.

It was a full-time job to raise teenagers, but I didn't want us to separate. I'm actually glad that task was left for me to do; it was a learning experience.

In dealing with the death of my mother, I had so much anger and hurt on the inside. My mother kept the family together; she was the one who with the ideas of what we could do together as a family. After her death, most of my siblings went their own ways. As I mentioned, I was difficult to get along with when I was grieving, and no one wanted to be around me. I took my mother's death out on them, as if they had something to do with her death.

When I got off work, I came home screaming, cussing, and getting into arguments with everyone. It didn't matter who it was as long as I could release my frustration on someone. That was my way of showing how angry I was, and the guilt just ate away at me.

Crying didn't help and talking to someone didn't help. That bitterness took over, and I took it out on my family.

Life for me was getting worse instead of better, maybe because I was still living in the house where she died. It wasn't just that I could still detect her scent. Her clothes also were still there—but she was gone. She was dead, but I kept waiting for her to walk in the door and tell me it was only a dream. I had this crazy idea that if I stayed up and waited for her, she'd come home. I waited and waited, but she never showed up, so I would call the hospital, just to see if they had a Cassandra Williams there. I thought maybe they would say, "Yes, she's here. Would you like her room number?" But instead, they said there was nobody by that name, even though I knew the whole time that she was dead. Again I thought this was a dream, but reality finally was beginning to sink in.

This took a toll on me, and at one point, I had to take sleeping pills to sleep or I'd cry myself to sleep. Staying in the same house where she died was not good for me at all. Those three years were so painful. I didn't want to move, because I still had hope that she would be back and wouldn't know where I'd gone. During those three years after she passed, I had to make myself get up and go to work. It was even harder for me on my days off. I would go to her grave and stay several hours, just talking, crying, and somehow hoping this was not real. After that, I would go back home, knowing she was dead but still looking for her to come home. Or I would sit at the hospital, waiting for her to call me to ask what time I would be coming up to her room, and when I did, would I bring her crossword puzzle book or personal items from home? But the call never came, so I would return home and cry myself to sleep.

During those three years after my mom's death, the pain was so intense that I finally had to move. I took her clothes and shoes with me. I needed something of hers, as I still wished and hoped this was only a dream. Logically, I knew she would not return, but I wasn't ready to let her go. Still, I knew I had to move on with my life, which was not easy at all. I had to let go, but I wasn't ready. I had to let go and let God, but I still wasn't ready. Her clothes gave me a sense of peace, knowing that she would always be part of me forever.

I still have these items in storage. I'm just not ready to give them away, and it's now going on nine years since she passed. I don't think I will ever be ready, but I'm in a much better place now than I was. Moving away from the house wasn't easy, but for me to move on, I had to leave that comfort zone. I had to leave the memories behind. I had to leave her scent behind. I had to leave it all behind for a fresh start.

Even with a fresh start, I'm still dealing with the loss and the guilt, depression, and pain. My heart still is so heavy because I feel like I left my best friend, my mother, behind without saying good-bye. My fresh start, however, helped me put a lot of things back in order. I slowly started praying again, asking God for strength, peace, and understanding and to help me get through this pain, guilt, and depression. I knew I couldn't do this by myself. He did exactly what I asked through my writing. With my book, I'm able share my story with those who might be dealing with the same issues or going through the same thing. I pray that those readers will find peace.

I eventually went back to school to get an associate of arts in human services management and will be receiving my bachelor's degree in early childhood education in 2015. I started a daycare in my house in 2010 to get those kids ready for school. Even though I had stopped praying and turned my back on God, blaming God for not answering my prayers the way I wanted him to, God was still right there with me the entire time.

God is a faithful God! Even though I went through a loss and it felt like God had failed me, God had my best interest at heart. God does everything for a reason. Yes, I still miss my mother, but I had to pick myself up and go on with my life.

6

Healing Process

The healing process not only meant personally dealing with my mother's death but also dealing with healing and mending broken relationships within my family. I said some things and went through a lot in my life over the past eight years, and now I was able to forgive and move on. Anger is a terrible thing to hold on to. Somebody dies every day, and I didn't want to wait until I was standing at a graveside to say I'm sorry or I love you.

I'm not perfect. I make mistakes, but it's never too late to ask God for help. Writing has helped me deal with my anger, depression, and guilt. While writing this book, I spent most of my days crying, trying to get past my mother's death and learning how to handle it. I have learned the best way to let it all out is to write it down on paper. This has helped me release a lot that was going on within me.

My own healing process has helped me reach out to my family to whom I haven't spoken in seven years. Through this, I have learned to cherish the moments with my loved ones. My advice to others is to make plenty of memories. Resolve differences because you never know when someone's life will be over.

I still get teary-eyed on my mom's birthday, on the anniversary date of her death, and especially during the holidays. I think about her smile and the love she showed all of her children. I think of how she helped people in a special way, such as praying for them, or calling to see how they were doing, or just offering a smile. A mother holds the most important place in a child's life. Mom was the only one who understood our tears, and she calmed our fears. Her death is something we will never get over, but slowly, we have learned to live with it.

Everyone grieves differently. I dealt with my grief in the only way I knew how, and that was with anger, getting in an unhealthy relationship, and being unable to let go of the house where my mother died.

The hardest thing I ever have had to deal with is losing my mother. She meant the world to me. She was only forty-four years old when she died. I was certain she would be on this earth longer than forty-four years, but it didn't happen like that. Her forty-four years weren't always good, but she lived life to the fullest, especially toward the end of her life. She still believed in God for her healing, and so did I. God did heal her, but not in the way I'd pray for.

I wanted God to heal my mother here on earth, not take her away. I know that might sound selfish, but I never thought it would turn out this way. "Weeping may endure for a night, but joy cometh in the morning" (Psalm 30:5). For me, joy came three years after my mother's death. I got my smile back, I found peace, and I started praying again.

If you have suffered a loss and think that joy will never return, I want to encourage you to keep trusting and believing in God. Through the pain, hurt, guilt, depression, and anger, God gave me enough grace to carry me through this situation. Even when God's answer is no or he has something better than what I've asked, I still trust him. His Grace is sufficient.

The healing process, for me, is going through the fire, but I came out without any burns, ashes, or scars. I'm still standing strong and depending, trusting, and believing in God, more than ever. Every year, when the anniversary of Mom's death comes, instead of going back to that dark place where I once resided, I ask God for strength, comfort, and peace, and I thank him for his grace. God's grace is sufficient.

Transformation Poem

With my head up, tears in my eyes, I will overcome the pain, guilt, depression, and hurt.

With my head up, tears in my eyes, I will smile again.

With my head up, tears in my eyes, I will trust God.

With my head up, tears in my eyes, a new chapter of my life begins.

With my head up, tears in my eyes, God's grace is sufficient.

With my head up, tears in my eyes, the healing begins.

With my head up, tears in my eyes, shouting, "Thank you, God, for strength, comfort, and peace."

With my head up, as God catches my tears,
with all the pain over the years.

With my head up, tears in my eyes, as I get my
faith back, as I get my life back on track.

With my head up, tears in my eyes, as I no
longer grieve while I started to read Romans
8:18. "For I reckon that the sufferings of
this present time are not worthy to be
compared with the glory which shall be
revealed in us."

7

Dedications

That's my grandmother. We did a lot together, from her taking me on errands with her, to going out to eat, just the two of us. We did almost everything together. If she was going somewhere, I was right there behind her. The way we were together, you'd think she was my mother riding around. She was one of the nicest people I've ever met in my life. She did a lot for me as I was growing up. I used to be her "road dog"—that's what she called me as we were riding. All that came to an end too soon. We didn't ride as much anymore, because I had to start school. She was like a second mom to me. We were really close. As I got older, I learned more and more about life. I prayed every day that God would heal her.

I didn't really know what was going on with her and her health problems. I just thought that she was sick and would get better. I continue to pray for her and her healing. That Saturday morning, my mom went to work. I was sitting in the living room with my grandmother. She didn't want to take her medicine. My aunt told me to check on her, and my grandmother was not breathing. Everyone started to freak out, and I knew something was wrong—she had died. I walked into my room and cried. Not only was she my grandmother, but she was like a second mother to me, and I miss her dearly.

I love you, Cat.

Continue to rest in peace.

Eric Wade

We were all so young, but we still understood what was happening. Pain is a concept that even the simplest creature on earth can understand. I'll bet I was as enraged as I could be with my grandmother's death. For the longest time, I stopped believing in God. It wasn't until recently, when I started going to the Fully Rely on God (FROG) club, that I understood that God would help me through things. Eight years later, I'm now twelve, and my brothers are ten, nine, and three. We're all going about our lives as normal kids who have coped and are continuing to cope with the loss of a loved one.

Love always,

Jennifer, Joshua, Caleb, and Jalen

I miss our mom so much. When she walked in a room, she warmed everybody's heart. She had a sweet spirit and a sweet smile. She loved God with all her heart. She loved all her children. That day when she died, I held her hand. I wanted her to wake up, but she wouldn't. Every night, Mom used to pray over all of us while we slept.

We would have Bible study at home, and she would ask each of us to read a verse from the Bible and tell what it meant. Mom had a beautiful voice. She lead the youth choir at church when we were in school. She made it to everything that was going on at our school. I miss her presence so much. If I could have one thing in this world, I would love to have our mom back, so she could see that we've grown up to be the beautiful men and women that she taught us to be. We love you.

Love,

Your daughter Lilly

On October 8, 2005, I lost the most important person in my life, my mother. I never thought she would leave me so soon. The day she passed away really hurt me so much. I didn't want to go on without her in my life. I wanted to give up. I know she is in a better place, watching over all her children. I miss you, Mom, so much. You still have a place in my heart, and I love you.

Love,

Your daughter Grace

On October 8, 2005, as I was leaving for work, I promised you that I would get off early so I could come back home and see after you. It never crossed my mind that *that* morning would be the last time I would talk with you. If I had known, I would never have gone to work. I would have stayed with you, holding your hand while you took your last breath.

Since then, I have dealt with a lot of guilt and a lot of what if's. The most hurtful thing about this is that I didn't even get to say goodbye. It still hurts, but I know that all that has happened is God's work, and I know that God did not take my mother without reason. I am still missing my mom.

Cherish those you love. I'd give all that I own to have her back with me. The pain never fades away.

Love always,
Your daughter Cassandra

Eight years—a long time. I miss the love of my life, my mom. She raised eight children, and when I say "raised," she did just that. Many memories—she made a way for all of her children. She made sure we didn't do without. She was a Christian woman, a God-fearing woman. I remember on some weekends, she would work from 11:00 p.m. until 7:00 a.m. and still have time to go to church on Sunday. Growing up, I don't think we missed a Sunday at church. I really miss the love, her smile, our talks, and most of all, the advice she gave. I remember the day before it all happened; she was in so much pain. I asked God to take care of her. On October 8, 2005, when my mom passed, I couldn't shake the confused look on my face or the pain I felt, but I know God makes no mistakes. Thank you, God, for giving me twenty-two years with the most wonderful person I know, my mother.

Continue to rest in peace, my love.

Forever in my heart,

Delmarcus

I appreciate my sister Cassandra D. Wade for taking time to write about our mom, Cassandra T. Wade. I told my sister Cassandra that writing the book is the best way to let the pain and emotions and stress out. We also hope this book will help a lot of people stay close with their families and not take things for granted. You never know when you will lose a loved one.

I was the sixth child in the family, born in October 1987. Growing up, I was the black sheep in the family, always trying to be different. When it came down to household rules, homework, and curfew, Mom didn't play. She always encouraged us as a family to finish school, stay out of trouble, and achieve the impossible. She was a great mother and granny. She always took care of us and told us that she loved us and God loved us. She took time to pray with us. I thank God for my mom's disciplining us when we were growing up.

I love her for trying her best with me because without her, I could be in prison or dead. In my later teenage years, I can remember my mom's directing the youth choir. This was around the time when she first got sick. For a while, we didn't know what was going on. Mom finally told us she had cancer. At the time, I didn't know what to think of the situation. Mom started going to the hospital a lot for her chemotherapy. One day, Mom said, "I believe in God," and she chose to stop going for treatments. I remember we used to pray in groups at home, in our prayer circles, hoping she would get better, but the cancer took complete control of her. Mom went from walking to sitting in a wheelchair full time.

Her feet used to hurt; they were swollen from fluids.

At Mom's ending stages of cancer, she couldn't recognize what was around her. She was in her own world. I tried to feed her plenty of times, but she couldn't eat; she was always in pain. I do thank God for Debra Webb for taking care of my mom. I'd like to thank the Elzie and Turner families for their help.

The cancer got worse, and hospice tried to offer comfort to my mom in her last days on earth. The only thing I regret is leaving the house before my mom's passing. I just couldn't take seeing the pain she was in. It was the type of pain that would make you break down in tears. I felt like it was driving me insane. I went to a friend's house to clear my head for a couple days, and during that time, my mom passed away. My brother found me and gave me the news that Mom was gone. I just couldn't believe that I wasn't there with her.

Her wake fell on my birthday, and then the next day was the funeral. I knew this would be the last time I would see her. She is resting now in a better place.

Thanks again, Mom, for believing in me when I didn't believe in myself.

Jeremy

I miss my mother very much. The things that I miss about her are her smile, her words of encouragement and endearment, her love for her kids and others, and her zeal for God. She was a woman of integrity and valor, and she was a woman after God's own heart. The impact that she left on her children and others is immense. She was the perfect example of how a woman should be. When she was alive, she had a heart of forgiveness and reconciliation. She had a heart of love like Jesus Christ. Jesus lived within her. Near the end of her life, she suffered greatly, but she never stopped believing in God. She believed in God even until death. Her living and suffering was not in vain. Death has no sting, because for her, to live was for Christ, and she gained a lot in death, which is to live eternally with Christ in the great coming day of our Lord. To be absent from the body is to be present with the Lord.

Love always,

Derriel

To my mother: words cannot express how I feel. On October 8, 2005, when they told me you had passed, I thought it wasn't true. I started to cry and kept saying to myself that somebody must be playing a joke on me. I had just talked to you during that week, and you told me not to worry about you, because you were going to be okay. Even though it's been eight years, the pain is still there. I miss you so much. Even my children say at times that they wish you were here, and it bring tears to my eyes, but I know you are in a better place, where the pain is no longer there. But the hurt remains.

I miss the advice you gave us daily and your unconditional love. I miss the fun times we had as a family—the laughs, the talks, and especially seeing your smile. Since your passing, there is a void in all of our lives that can never be filled. We will meet again. Until then, I just keep the memories close. You are truly missed by me and your grandchildren.

Love you always,

Lakesha

Mom, during those times when my wife took you to the hospital and saw you in so much pain, it broke my heart. On October 8, 2005, when I received the call that told me you had passed, my heart dropped. I felt like I couldn't breathe. I was so overwhelmed with tears that I had to come and see for myself if it was really true—that my angel, my sweetheart, my mother had passed. When I arrived at the house, I still couldn't believe you were gone. Do I understand? No! Will I ever understand? No! Are you suffering anymore? No! I thank God that you no longer are in any pain, but I miss you so much that my pain is still there.

Mom, your death affected all of your children in so many ways. We weren't ready to let go. I know you were in a lot of pain, and you went through a lot of pain from chemo. God, I thank you for those wonderful years that my mother was with all of her children and grandchildren.

Cassandra T. Williams, you will always be in our hearts and we truly miss you.

Love always,

Donald

A special tribute to Cassandra Teresa Turner Wade-Williams…

"As We Knew Her"

From the start, Cassandra was a shining star. A beautiful baby girl, attracting attention from all who came in contact with her.

Cassandra, or Songa, as she was affectionately called, lived her life with passion, generosity, compassion, sincerity, love, joy, and faith. She loved life and life in the form of family, friends, and coworkers. This exuberance was her ministry. Everyone she met was attracted to her personality, and she was always helping somebody. She gave her life to Christ at an early age but really committed totally to him as an adult and was faithful in the ministry. We thank God for the gift placed in our lives and the impact and legacy she left with us. We look forward to the time we will all see and rejoice in the Lord together again, celebrating our Lord Jesus.

Love forever and always,

Your mother, Queen Esther Raye Jackson, and your siblings, Esther, Susan, Darryl, Cheryl, Aretha, and Lana Turner

How priceless is your unfailing love, O God!
People take refuge in the shadow of your
    wings.
They feast on the abundance of your house;
you give them drink from your river of delights.
For with you is the fountain of life; in your
    light we see light.
Continue your love to those who know you,
    your righteousness to the upright in heart.
—Psalm 36:7–10